Dedicated to all who love numbers!

All rights reserved.
No part of this book may be reproduced in any form or by any means, electronic or mechanical, and no photocopying or recording, unless you have written permission from the author.

ISBN 978-1-958985-06-9

Copyright © 2024 by Mimi Jones

www.joeysavestheday.com

A Mimi Book

Zero

One

Two

Three

Four

Five

Six

Seven

Eight

Nine

Ten

Eleven

Twelve

Thirteen

Fourteen

Fifteen

Go learn
some big numbers.

The End!

About the author:

Mimi is a homeschool mom of two. She loves to draw, read, and write. Mimi reside on the east coast with her guitar playing husband.

Please Check out her other great books on Amazon.

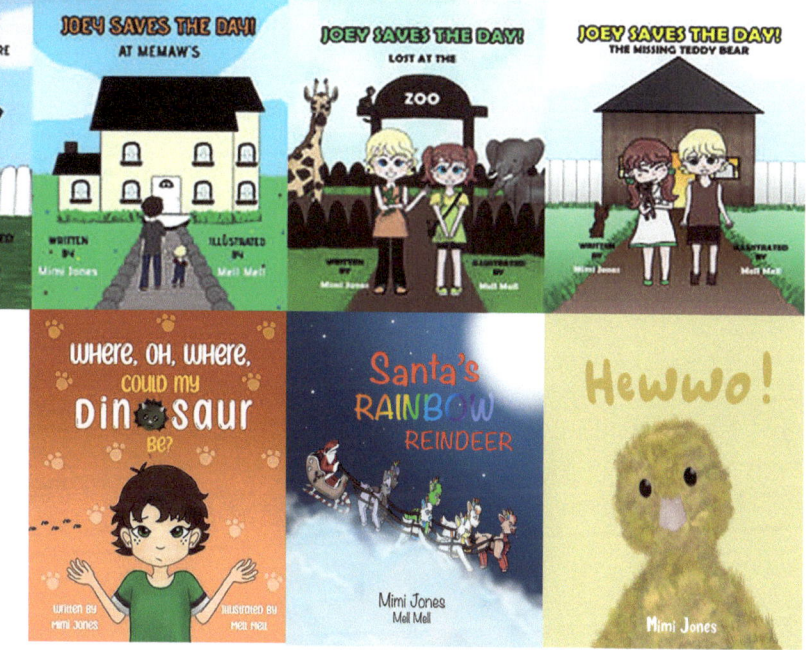

www.joeysavestheday.com

www.ingramcontent.com/pod-product-compliance
Lightning Source LLC
Chambersburg PA
CBHW040027050426
42453CB00002B/26